Star-struck Tom

Tom was watching TV.
He was watching a big
tennis star.

3

"I can be a big tennis star," said Tom. "I can be on TV."

"No," said Kim. "You can't be on TV."

DON'T DROP IT!

Contents

Jeremy Taylor

Story illustrated by
Steve May

Heinemann

In this story

 Tom

 Kim

 TV man

Tricky words

- watching
- tennis star
- racket
- balls
- juggling

Introduce these tricky words and help the reader when they come across them later!

Story starter

Tom likes watching sport on TV. One day, he was watching a big tennis star on TV. Tom wanted to be a TV tennis star too, but his racket was too old.

Tom got out his old tennis racket and his old tennis balls.

Tom played tennis.

He played every day.

He played and played.

"You can't be a tennis star," said Kim.
"Your tennis racket is too old."

Tom looked at his tennis balls. "But I **can** be a juggling star," he said.

So Tom juggled every day.

He juggled and juggled.

A TV man was watching
Tom juggle.

"You can juggle," he said.
"You can be on TV."

So Tom was on TV.
Kim said, "You are a
juggling star!"

Would you like to be on TV?

Quiz

Text Detective

- Why did Tom get out his old tennis racket?
- What sport would you like to be really good at?

Word Detective

- Phonic Focus: Blending three phonemes
  Page 9: Can you sound out 'can'?
- Page 5: Find a word that rhymes with 'shout'.
- Page 8: Find a word that is the opposite of 'new'.

Super Speller

Read these words:

played   man   day

Now try to spell them!

HA! HA! HA!

Q What's a horse's favourite sport?

A Stable tennis.

13

Before Reading

Find out about

- How to juggle
- Some crazy juggling stunts

Tricky words

- start
- juggling
- right
- throw
- catch
- crazy
- stilts

Introduce these tricky words and help the reader when they come across them later!

Text starter

Learn how to juggle with three juggling balls. You will have to throw the juggling balls from your right hand to your left hand. Then read about some crazy juggling.

How to Juggle

Start with two juggling balls in your right hand, and one juggling ball in your left hand.

Throw one juggling ball
from your right hand.
Catch it in your left hand.

Throw one juggling ball from your left hand. Catch it in your right hand.

Now, throw the juggling balls again.

Throw from your right hand to your left hand and from your left hand to your right hand.

But before you catch the juggling ball in your right hand, throw the other juggling ball from your right hand.

Catch the juggling ball in your left hand, then start again.

Crazy Juggling

Look at this crazy juggling!
Would you try to juggle with
bananas?

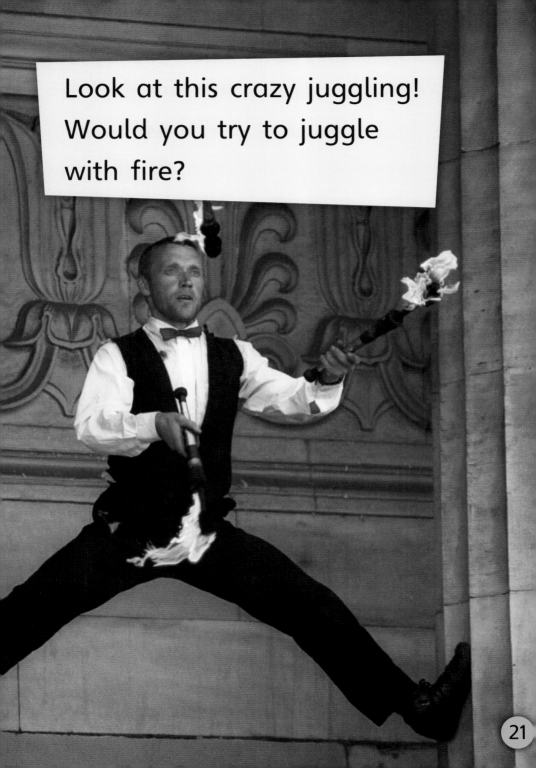

Look at this crazy juggling!
Would you try to juggle
with fire?

Look at this crazy juggling! Would you try to juggle with tables ...

What else could you juggle with?